Rob's mum
Pen
Spot

Is Rob in?
Is he in?

Yes

Yes, Rob is in.

He is in bed.

Rob is up in bed.

Rob. It is Pen.

No!

Pen went up.

Spot went up.

Pen and Spot
went up to Rob.

Pen and Spot
went up to help Rob.

Can I help,
Rob?

No!

Up...
...down!
Up...
...down!

I can help Spot.

Spot likes Rob.

Rob likes Spot.
Spot likes Rob!